EMERG 999!

SEA RESCUE SERVICES

Kathryn Walker

Photography by Chris Fairclough

WAYLAND

Published in 2013 by Wayland

Copyright © Wayland 2013

Wayland
338 Euston Road
London NW1 3BH

Wayland Australia
Level 17/207 Kent Street
Sydney, NSW 2000

Produced for Wayland by Discovery Books Ltd
Wayland series editor: Katie Powell
Editor: James Nixon
Designer: Ian Winton
Commissioned photography: Chris Fairclough

The author, publisher and Discovery Books Ltd would like to thank the Royal National
Lifeboat Institution for their help and participation in this book.

Picture credits: Getty Images: p. 13 bottom (Digital Vision); Maritime and Coastguard
Agency: pp. 4 top, 6, 7, 8, 9 top, 10, 11, 12, 23, 25, 31; RNLI: pp. 9 bottom, 15 top, 16, 17 middle,
18 middle and bottom, 20, 21, 22, 26, 27; Shutterstock: pp. 4 bottom, 24 (Eric Gevaert), 28 top
(Larry St. Pierre), 28 bottom (Rob Wilson), 29 top, 29 bottom (Alex Jackson).

British Library Cataloguing in Publication Data
Walker, Kathryn, 1957-
   Sea rescue services. -- (Emergency 999)
   1. Lifeboat service--Juvenile literature.
   I. Title II. Series
   363.1'2381-dc22
   ISBN: 978 0 7502 7882 9

Printed in China

10 9 8 7 6 5 4 3 2 1

Wayland is a division of Hachette Children's Books,
an Hachette UK company. www.hachette.co.uk

Note to parents and teachers: Every effort has been made by the Publishers to ensure that
the websites in this book are suitable for children, that they are of the highest educational
value, and that they contain no inappropriate or offensive material. However, because of the
nature of the Internet, it is impossible to guarantee that the contents of these sites will not be
altered. We strongly advise that Internet access is supervised by a responsible adult.

CONTENTS

CALL THE COASTGUARD!

A day at the seaside, a boat trip or a walk along the coast can be fun. But sea, rocks, mud and cliffs can be dangerous, too.

People and animals sometimes fall down cliffs or become trapped when the **tide** comes in. Children on lilos can get blown out to sea. When accidents like this happen, how do we get help?

The coastguard is an emergency service that helps people in trouble at the coast. This includes people who fall into the water.

If you see someone in trouble at sea, on the cliffs or on the **shoreline**, phone 999. An operator will answer your call and ask which emergency service you need. Ask for the coastguard.

Help centres

The coastguard is responsible for getting help to people in the sea and on the shoreline of the United Kingdom. It controls search and rescue (SAR) operations from 19 centres around the coast. These are called Maritime Rescue Co-ordination Centres.

You will need to tell the coastguard:
- what the problem is
- where the problem is and where you are phoning from
- when the **incident** took place
- your name.

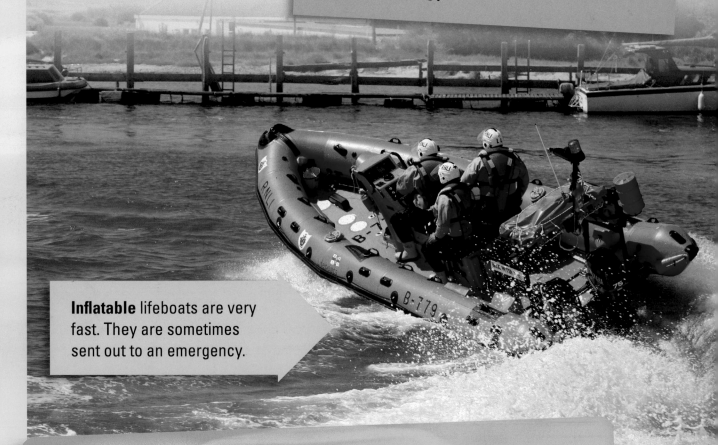

Inflatable lifeboats are very fast. They are sometimes sent out to an emergency.

999 Notes

If you see a swimmer in trouble in the sea, do not go into the water to rescue them. You could put yourself in danger and then need rescuing yourself. Instead, find the nearest **lifeguard** or phone the coastguard.

SENDING HELP

Your emergency telephone call to the coastguard is put through to the nearest Maritime Rescue Co-ordination Centre. At these centres, teams of coastguard operators use computers, charts and radios to organise help.

Maritime Rescue Co-ordination Centre

When you report your emergency, coastguard operators decide what type of help is needed. They may send out helicopters, lifeboats or land-rescue teams – sometimes all three.

Operators stay in touch with the teams throughout a rescue, making sure everyone knows what to do and has all the information they need.

A useful tool

Coastguard operators have a special computer system to help them plan searches. This uses information on tides and winds to work out where rescuers should look if a boat or person at sea has drifted away.

Computers are a vital tool in a coastguard centre, but officers also use telescopes to watch over the local coastline.

FACE-TO-FACE

Fiona – Coastguard Watch Officer

I work at a rescue co-ordination centre where I answer 999 telephone calls. When there is an emergency, I work with my **watch manager** to send out search and rescue (SAR) teams.

I spend some of my time gathering information about tides and weather. I need to use lots of different types of equipment, so there's always something new to learn.

COASTGUARD RESCUE TEAMS

In an emergency, the coastguard may send out a Coastguard Rescue Team to help. This is a team of **volunteer** coastguards trained to carry out search and rescue along the coast and cliffs. The teams are also trained in giving **first aid** to injured people.

Getting there quickly

These volunteers may be called out to an emergency at any time of day or night. They carry **pagers** – devices that bleep to let them know when they are needed. To help them get to an emergency fast they use off-road vehicles for travelling over rough ground and beaches.

A Coastguard Rescue Team is made up of at least 11 people who live locally and know the coastline well.

Coastguard vehicles have blue flashing lights and sirens. These warn other motorists to let them through.

Volunteers never know when they will be called out so they always carry some pieces of equipment with them. These include a radio, a torch, a helmet and boots for walking or climbing.

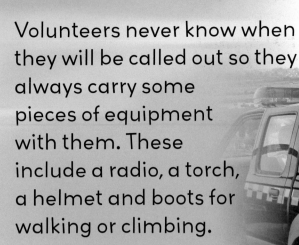

The Coastguard Rescue Team's off-road vehicle has room in the boot for storing the rescue equipment.

999 Notes

Coastguard Rescue Teams are sometimes called out to investigate unusual objects that have been washed up on the shore. Sometimes these turn out to be unexploded sea **mines**. The teams are also called to help rescue **stranded** whales, dolphins or seals.

A stranded dolphin, like this one, will get help from lifeboat teams and Coastguard Rescue Teams.

MUD AND CLIFF RESCUE

The coastguard is often called to help when people or animals have fallen down cliffs or are stuck in mud or **quicksand**. Depending on the type of coastline in their area, volunteer coastguards are trained in mud or cliff rescue.

Sledges and pumps

Mud rescue teams sometimes use a sledge to rescue people or animals. The sledge slides across the mud or quicksand and has a rope attached to the shore. Sticky mud can hold people tight, so rescuers may use a mud lance. This pumps water or air into the mud under the trapped person, making it easier to free them.

mud lance

sledge

A mud rescue team pull a man to safety. A person can quickly sink up to the neck in mud or quicksand.

harness

Ropes and winches

To reach someone who is trapped or injured on a cliff side, a rescuer is lowered down on a rope. The rescuer puts the person on a stretcher or in a harness. Other team members then haul them to safety using a **winch**.

Cliff rescue teams are specially trained in using ropes, harnesses and other climbing equipment.

FACE-TO-FACE

Roger – Volunteer Coastguard

I work as an electrician, but I'm a volunteer coastguard, too. I can be called to an emergency at any time. It could be to search for a missing person or to rescue someone trapped on a cliff side.

The team meets at evenings and weekends to train. I get a small payment for a call-out, but that's not why I do this job. I do it because I like to be out there helping people.

MAYDAY!

Boats and ships sometimes get into difficulties at sea. This could be because of bad weather, engine problems or because someone on board is very ill. In these emergencies, sailors or crews call the coastguard.

Signs of trouble

Most **vessels** use radio or telephone 999 to call for help. If these are not working, there are other ways of letting people know that a boat is in trouble. One way is to send up a **flare** with a red light or orange smoke. Sounding a **foghorn** continuously is another way to signal for help.

All sea vessels must have a way of contacting the coastguard to report an accident or danger.

Some vessels carry a special device called a distress radio beacon. This sends a signal via a **satellite** to the nearest rescue co-ordination centre to let them know they need help. The signal helps rescuers locate the vessel.

Distress radio beacons like this have saved many lives. The radio signals they send tell rescuers the exact location of the vessel or person that needs help.

999 Notes

When a boat is in trouble, a crew member can radio for help using the emergency code word 'Mayday'. This word is only used when people's lives are in danger. Over the radio, the caller says 'Mayday' three times in a row then gives the vessel's name and position. The word 'Mayday' comes from the French 'M'aider' or 'M'aidez', meaning 'come and help me'.

LIFEBOATS

All along the coastline, lifeboat stations have boats ready to help people in trouble. When the coastguard wants a lifeboat to go to an incident, they contact lifeboat crew members on pagers. The crew and helpers quickly make their way to their local lifeboat station.

pager

The main lifeboat service is the Royal National Lifeboat Institution (RNLI). Lifeboats are paid for through **donations**. The crews and helpers are all volunteers.

Inshore lifeboats are used for emergencies close to shore. These light, inflatable boats usually carry a crew of three.

Inshore lifeboats can get to places that are difficult to reach, such as among rocks, in caves or close to cliffs.

All-weather lifeboats (left) are bigger. They have a crew of six and go into deeper waters.

All-weather lifeboats are designed to be able to operate in severe weather conditions.

FACE-TO-FACE

Andy – Lifeboat Crew Member

When my pager goes off I have to get to the lifeboat station within five minutes – even if I'm in bed! Our station has an inshore lifeboat and I am the **helmsman**. This means that when we go out, I'm in charge of the boat and crew.

We meet regularly at evenings and weekends to train and practise, to check equipment and to plan. I enjoy working as part of a close team and being able to help people.

AT THE LIFEBOAT STATION

Each lifeboat station has a boathouse where the lifeboat or lifeboats are kept. Some stations have tractors to tow their lifeboat to and from the water. In stations where the water is deep, there is a ramp down from which the boat is launched.

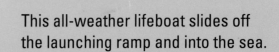

This all-weather lifeboat slides off the launching ramp and into the sea.

999 Notes

Shore helpers are volunteers that work in a lifeboat station but do not go out in the boats. Some help launch the boats or are mechanics who look after the boats. Others help with the day-to-day running of the station.

A place to meet

The station has a room where the crew meet and hold training sessions (left). There are also toilets and showers for the crew, and storerooms where equipment and medical supplies are kept.

Special kit

The crew keep their protective clothing by the lifeboat so they can slip into it quickly when there is a call-out. The kit includes:

outer dry suit to keep out the water

helmet, often with an inbuilt radio

life jacket, with pockets for torches, flares and other equipment

All-weather lifeboat crews wear yellow waterproof trousers and jackets instead of dry suits. Unlike the inshore crews, they do not need to stand in the water to launch and recover their boats.

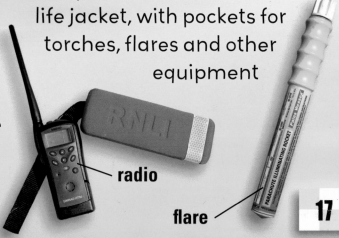

radio

flare

LIFEBOAT RESCUE

When there is an emergency call-out, the lifeboat crew go to the station, get dressed and gather the equipment they need. Someone speaks to the coastguard by radio and passes on details of who is going out on the lifeboat (right).

An inflatable lifeboat quickly sets off to answer an emergency call.

Keeping in touch

When the crew reach the emergency scene, they radio the coastguard to let them know that they have arrived. Some rescues are completed quickly; some can take hours. Other help may be involved, such as helicopter rescue.

On a helicopter rescue, the different crews need to communicate with each other as well as the coastguard.

Back to base

When the lifeboat returns, it is towed back up the beach or winched up the ramp.

At some lifeboat stations, a tractor is used to pull the lifeboat back on to dry land after a call-out.

The boats, tractor and trailer have to be hosed down with fresh water (left). This is because salt water makes things rust. The equipment is checked over and the fuel tank filled. Then the lifeboat is ready for the next call-out.

999 Notes

Lifeboat crews need lots of training and practice. They need to know how to work and communicate with helicopters and how to rescue people from the water. Crew members must also practise giving first aid and using radio equipment. They do a lot of training at the lifeboat stations, but they may also train at the Lifeboat College in Poole, Dorset.

LIFEGUARDS

Lots of people enjoy spending a day at the beach, especially in the summer. But every year, swimmers, surfers and small children get into difficulties at the seaside. To make sure they get help fast, the RNLI has lifeguards working on many UK beaches throughout the summer months.

Keeping watch

Lifeguards are trained in water rescue and first aid. They also advise people on how to stay safe at the beach. The lifeguards **patrol** the area or keep watch from a **lookout**.

Lifeguards use a raised area with a good view of the beach as a lookout.

On the water

Lifeguards have inflatable rescue boats and rescue water crafts to go out on to the water.

Lifeguards use inflatable rescue boats to get to a swimmer quickly.

jet ski

A rescue water craft, also called a jet ski (left), looks a bit like a scooter and has a sled attached for bringing people to safety. Sometimes, the fastest way for a lifeguard to reach someone is to use a type of surfboard called a rescue board.

FACE-TO-FACE

Emma – Beach Lifeguard

I'm a student, but I work as a lifeguard during the summer. Sometimes I help swimmers in difficulty or people who have drifted out to sea on body boards or inflatables. I also spend a lot of time helping to find lost children and warning people of dangers.

I enjoy being a lifeguard. It's a great way to spend the summer holidays and it keeps me fit.

AIR RESCUE

Emergencies at sea or along the coast sometimes need the help of a helicopter. This might be to search for people or to airlift them to safety. The coastguard has its own search and rescue (SAR) helicopters, but can also call Royal Navy and Royal Air Force helicopters to go to an emergency.

Helicopter crew

A coastguard helicopter carries four crew members – two pilots, a **winchman** and a winch operator. The winchman goes down on a wire to rescue people. The winch operator is in charge of lowering and raising the winchman and also the people being rescued.

The work of a sea rescue helicopter crew takes a lot of skill and training. It can be very dangerous, especially in bad weather.

winchman

Special equipment

Helicopters carry video and **thermal imaging cameras** to help them find people. These cameras can form an image from the heat that a body gives off. This makes them very useful for finding people, especially in the dark.

FACE-TO-FACE

Kevin – SAR Helicopter Pilot

At the beginning of a shift, we plan the day's training. We do practice flights, but no more than four hours flying training a day. Any more would leave us too tired to cope with a real emergency.

When there's a call-out, we have to be in the air within 15 minutes. It can be dangerous work when the weather is bad, but I love flying and working with the team.

23

NON-EMERGENCY WORK

Answering emergency calls and organising rescues is just a part of the work that coastguard officers do. A lot of their time is spent gathering and giving out information to help people keep safe at sea.

People may ring or radio the coastguard to ask for information or advice on safety matters. Every four hours, coastguard officers broadcast safety information over the radio. This includes weather forecasts for sea and coastal areas, as well as warnings of **gales**.

Bad weather can put sailors and crews in great danger.

On the lookout

Coastguard officers keep watch over the coastline and go out on patrol. They check that vessels are not breaking the law by carrying **cargo** that is not allowed into the country. Officers also look out for vessels that are not obeying safety rules.

Coastguard officers go out on patrol, watching out for lawbreakers and dangers in the water.

A coastguard officer uses an off-road vehicle to patrol a beach and scans the coastline for signs of trouble.

Saving the sea

After an accident at sea, there is sometimes a risk of **pollution**. For example, dangerous chemicals or oil might escape into the sea. When this happens, coastguard teams work to clean up the area and to stop the pollution spreading.

SPREADING THE WORD

Lifeboat and Coastguard Rescue Teams work hard to rescue people, but they are also busy trying to prevent accidents happening. Part of their work is to visit schools. They give talks to explain what they do and teach young people how to stay safe in and near the sea.

Lifeguards teach children surf skills and beach safety.

Demonstrating skills

Lifeboat crews also give public demonstrations of their search and rescue skills. This helps to make people aware of how important the lifeboat service is and of the need to raise money to keep it going. The demonstrations also encourage people to think about joining their local lifeboat service, either as crew members or shore helpers.

Fund-raising

The money needed to run lifeboat services comes from donations and it is important to make sure the money keeps coming in. Some people help their local lifeboat service by becoming volunteer fund-raisers. They work hard to find ways of raising money and by organising different events. These might be sponsored swims or runs, or family fun days.

Surfers in Cornwall bring ashore a giant inflatable bottle to advertise the RNLI's appeal for donations.

In 2010, lifeboat crew members raised money by taking part in the London Marathon. As they ran they carried a pretend lifeboat.

999 Notes

The RNLI has a club for children called Storm Force. Members receive badges and a magazine with lifeboat news, stories and competitions. It costs a few pounds a year to join and this money goes towards running the lifeboat service.

STAYING SAFE

To make sure your trip to the coast is a safe one, be aware of the dangers and follow some basic safety rules. The first rule is not to go near the sea on your own and to make sure others know where you are going.

Ask an adult to check the latest information on the weather and tides for the area you are visiting. The weather can change very quickly and tides can be a hazard.

Lots of people enjoy a sunny day at the beach, but every year thousands get into trouble.

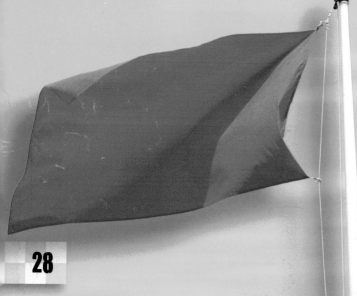

Flag alert

At the beach, look out for danger signs and flags. Red flags warn that the water is unsafe. Red and yellow flags show areas where it is safe to swim. Black and white flags indicate an area for boats and surfers – this is not an area for swimmers.

Inflatable trouble

If you are using an inflatable, such as a dinghy or lilo, be very careful. They can easily carry you into deep waters. An inflatable should always have a rope attached for someone on shore to hold on to. Never take one out when there are strong winds or large waves.

Inflatables like this can be dangerous. They should only be used with the help of an adult.

999 Notes

If you get into trouble when swimming, try to stay calm and float on your back. Keep breathing steadily. To attract attention, wave one arm and shout for help.

Signs and flags at the beach give important safety information. Make sure you know what they mean.

DO YOU HAVE WHAT IT TAKES?

Anyone who wants to become a lifeboat crew member needs to live or work close to a lifeboat station. It is not full-time work, so crew members often have other jobs that may have nothing to do with the sea or boats. You must be over 18, or over 17 and have your parents' permission.

First, you will have medical and eyesight tests to make sure you are fit to do the work. If everything is fine, you are put 'on probation' for a year. This means that for one year you train to become a crew member. Then, if you have done well and other crew members are happy to work with you, you become a full member of the lifeboat crew.

Could you be a lifeboat crew member?
Look at the following questions and answer 'yes' or 'no'.

- Do you live on the coast?
- Are you willing to go out to an emergency at any time of the day or night and often in bad weather?
- Are you happy to give up your spare time during the week or at weekends to train and practise?
- Can you stay calm in a dangerous situation?
- Are you happy to do hard, physical work?
- Do you work well as part of a team?
- Would you be happy to talk to people about your work and help with fund-raising?

If you answered 'yes' to all these questions, then maybe you do have what it takes to be a lifeboat crew member.

GLOSSARY

cargo goods carried on a ship or other vehicle

donation something that is given as a gift to a charity or organisation

first aid the emergency care given to a sick or injured person before skilled medical help is available

flare a device that produces a bright fire or light, used as a signal

foghorn a device on a ship that makes a loud, deep sound as a warning signal

gale strong wind

helmsman a person who steers a ship or boat

incident something that happens

inflatable describes something that can be filled up with air

lifeguard an expert swimmer employed to rescue people who get into difficulty at the beach

lookout a place that gives a lifeguard a good view of their surroundings

mine an explosive that is hidden under the ground or at sea

pager a small device that bleeps or vibrates to let you know that someone wishes to contact you

patrol to move about a particular area, watching and checking that all is well

pollution substances that dirty or poison the air, land or water

quicksand loose, wet sand that sucks in anything that lands on it

satellite a machine sent into space to orbit the Earth. It can send and receive radio signals

shoreline the water's edge, where it meets the land

stranded left in a helpless position, without a way to escape

thermal imaging camera a camera that forms an image from heat given off by objects. It can show an image of a person in the dark because the body gives off heat

tide the regular rise and fall of the sea

vessel a ship or large boat

volunteer a person who does a job for very little pay or no pay at all

watch manager someone responsible for planning the work of a team and watching over them

winch a machine used for lifting or hauling things

winchman a member of a helicopter crew who is lowered on a wire to rescue people and haul them to safety

INDEX AND FURTHER INFORMATION

Websites

This RNLI site for young people has lots of fun activities and games, a virtual tour of a lifeboat, interviews with crew members and lots more:
http://www.rnli.org.uk/Shorething/Youth/

This Coastguard (MCA) website has lots of safety information for children and teenagers, games and downloads:
http://www.mcga.gov.uk/c4mca/seasmart-home

The HM Coastguard Scarborough has this website with lots of pictures and information about their station, equipment and team and a special childen's section with games and activities: **http://www.scarboroughcoastguard.co.uk/**

Books

Call the Coastguard (In An Emergency), Cath Senker, Franklin Watts, 2010
Lifeboat Crew Member (People Who Help Us), Rebecca Hunter, Cherrytree Books, 2008
Rescue at Sea (People Who Help Us), Clare Oliver, Franklin Watts, 2006